The Battle of the Somme

World War One's Bloodiest Battle

Rupert Colley

Copyright © 2016 Rupert Colley
CreateSpace Edition

All rights reserved.
ISBN- 978-1532997921
1532997922

Rupert Colley was born one Christmas Day and grew up in Devon. A history graduate, he worked as a librarian in London before starting 'History In An Hour' – a series of non-fiction history ebooks that can be read in just sixty minutes, acquired by Harper Collins in 2011. He has also penned eight works of historical fiction. Now a full time writer, speaker and the author of historical novels, he lives in Waltham Forest, London with his wife, two children and dog.

Works by Rupert Colley:

Fiction:
My Brother the Enemy
The Black Maria
The Sixth Man
The Torn Flag
The Unforgiving Sea
The White Venus
The Woman on the Train
This Time Tomorrow

History In An Hour series:
1914: History In An Hour
Black History: History In An Hour
D-Day: History In An Hour
Hitler: History In An Hour
Mussolini: History In An Hour
Nazi Germany: History In An Hour
Stalin: History In An Hour
The Afghan Wars: History In An Hour
The Cold War: History In An Hour
The Russian Revolution: History In An Hour
The Siege of Leningrad: History In An Hour
World War One: History In An Hour
World War Two: History In An Hour

Other non-fiction:
The Savage Years: Tales From the 20th Century
A History of the World Cup: An Introduction

The Battle of the Somme

Historyinanhour.com
Rupertcolley.com

Table of Contents

Introduction	1
1914 – 1915	4
The Battle of Verdun	13
The Somme Offensive: Plans and Preparations	18
The First Day, Saturday 1 July 1916	30
2 July – 18 November 1916	49
The Battle is Over	78
Postscript	87
Other works by Rupert Colley	93

Introduction

The Battle of the Somme lives in our collective imagination as the epitome of pointless slaughter on the battlefield. It was one of the costliest engagements of the First World War and, a century on, the Somme has come to symbolize the futile horrors of trench warfare. The first day, 1 July 1916, was the worst, blackest day in British military history – 57,470 casualties, including 19,240 dead. The failure to breach the German lines on the first day led to a battle of attrition that was to last four and a half long months. By the time it had finished on 18 November, after 141 days of carnage, more than a million men had been killed or wounded on all sides, making it one of the bloodiest battles in human history.

The proposal for a major Anglo-French offensive near the River Somme was first suggested by the French commander-in-chief, Joseph Joffre, at the Chantilly Conference in December 1915. Representatives from France, Great Britain, Italy and Russia attended. Representing the British was commander-in-chief, Sir John French. (A week later, French was replaced as c-in-c by Sir Douglas Haig, whose name would soon become synonymous with the Battle of the Somme). The Germans, Joffre felt, were running out of reserves and a concentrated combined attack would provide the long-awaited breakthrough on the Western Front. The proposal was agreed. Originally, the French would have taken the lead, but on 21 February 1916, the Germans launched an all-out assault on the French town of Verdun. As a result, with the French embroiled at Verdun, they were reduced to a supporting role on the Somme. The brunt of the attack would fall on the forces of the British and its Commonwealth.

The British and Commonwealth had two main

objectives for the coming Somme offensive: firstly to relieve the pressure on the French at Verdun; and secondly, to breakthrough German lines and to 'inflict as heavy losses as possible upon the German armies,' to use Douglas Haig's phrase, and, using the cavalry, reinstate a war of movement.

The British however knew they lacked experienced men. Its professional army, the British Expeditionary Force, had almost been wiped out.

Re-enactment of Canadian troops 'going over the top', Battle of the Somme, 1916. Imperial War Museum.

1914 – 1915

In 1914, the BEF as a fighting force was highly trained, highly proficient but very small. Britain's European counterparts all had massive armies of conscripted soldiers. Britain, however, was against forcing unwilling men to take up arms – thus it relied on its professional army. With the outbreak of war, it soon became apparent that Britain needed a much larger army – an army of paid volunteers. So the government went on a recruitment campaign.

The newly-appointed Minister of War, Horatio Kitchener, a military hero and veteran of the Boer War, lent his face to the most popular of the many recruiting posters. With his military hat and stern face, his pointing finger jabbed at the conscience of the viewer – 'Your country needs you!' bellowed the poster.

*Horatio Herbert Kitchener, 1914.
Library of Congress.*

The campaign was hugely successful. Men (and boys) the length and breadth of the country queued at the various recruitment agencies, eager to sign on the dotted line and join up. For many, working class life was dull, monotonous and poorly paid. Here was a unique opportunity – the chance of seeing foreign lands, the possibility of adventure, some decent pay and the chance to impress people back home by their sense of patriotic duty. By the end of 1914, over a million young men, the 'Kitchener recruits', had volunteered.

(Horatio Kitchener drowned in the North Sea on 5 June 1916 when the ship he was on, the HMS *Hampshire*, hit a German mine. His body was never found).

British general, Henry Rawlinson, persuaded 1,500 London City workers to form a 'Stockbrokers' Battalion'. This was the first of what became known as 'pal battalions', when men could sign-up to serve alongside their friends, workmates or townsfolk. By the end of September 1914 almost sixty towns from across the UK had formed into battalions. 12,000 postal workers joined the Post Office Rifles battalion. The idea, which made sense on paper, proved disastrous. It meant that if a town's battalion was decimated, such as the Accrington Pals on the first day of the Somme, a whole town would be left bereft with grief as a large proportion of its menfolk were wiped out at once.

Once war had started, young men who had not joined up, for whatever reason, risked being presented with a white feather, a symbol of cowardice. The practice became so widespread that the military authorities had to issue special silver badges to soldiers who had been honourably discharged or men who worked in vital war work at home to distinguish them from 'shirkers'.

It takes time to train a raw recruit into something resembling a fully-fledged fighting machine – even during wartime when time is of the essence. So, while the mass of volunteers were being put through their paces, the BEF, starting on 7 August 1914, crossed the English Channel ready to fight. The German Kaiser, Wilhelm II, had reputably referred to the BEF as 'General French's contemptible little army'. The 'contemptible' may have referred to the size rather than the quality of Britain's army but nonetheless the BEF took perverse pride in calling themselves the 'old contemptibles'. It was on 23 August, near the small

Franco-Belgium border town of Mons, that the BEF met the German army and fought its first battle on European soil since Waterloo almost a century earlier. The BEF managed to hold its own for a while before being outnumbered and outgunned by the German advance and forced into a retreat.

Germany had long-prepared for a European war on two fronts. In 1894 and 1904, France, Russia and Great Britain had signed a set of treaties that had effectively bound them together in the event of war – the 'Triple Entente'. Germany was also part of a three-way agreement, the 'Triple Alliance', with the Austro-Hungarian Empire and Italy, signed in 1879 and 1882. Hence, the Germans were fully aware that if it came to war they faced the French to the west and the Russians to the east. And so in the years leading up to 1914 they prepared accordingly using as a blueprint a plan devised by the German chief-of-staff, Alfred von Schlieffen. The plan pre-supposed that Russia, given its size, both in territory and manpower, would take six weeks to fully mobilize for war. Thus the most effective way to deal with both enemies, according to von Schlieffen (who died in

1913), would be to invade France through Luxemburg and Belgium (even if it meant violating Belgium's neutrality which both Great Britain and Germany herself had guaranteed with a signing of a treaty in 1839), then arc southwards to capture Paris. With France knocked out, German troops could then march eastwards, back through Germany, to meet the Russian threat in time.

On 2 August, Germany invaded neutral Luxemburg, which would remain under German occupation until the end of the war. The German government then demanded passage through Belgium. On 3 August, Germany declared war on France. The following day, having been refused access, Germany invaded Belgium regardless, attacking the city of Liège. The resulting Battle of Liège was the first battle of the war. Britain demanded that Germany withdraw, determined to uphold its pledge to Belgium. Referring to the 1839 treaty, the German chancellor, Theobald von Bethmann-Hollweg, couldn't believe the British would wage war with a 'kindred spirit' over a 'scrap of paper'. Germany refused to withdraw and thus at 11 p.m. on

4 August, Britain declared war on Germany. Sir Edward Grey, Britain's foreign minister, gazing out from the Foreign Office windows, remarked, 'the lamps are going out all over Europe. We shall not see them lit again in our lifetime'.

Cavalry Division, British Expeditionary Force, on the Retreat from Mons, August 1914. Imperial War Museum.

Within three weeks the Germans had fought their way through Belgium (although it would take another couple of months to subdue Belgium entirely) and had reached Mons, which is where they met the determined BEF and forced the British army into what became known as the 'Retreat from Mons'.

By early September, the British had retreated 175 miles southwards under the hot August sun, managing only three hours sleep a night, the Germans never far behind them. Soon, Paris, only fourteen miles away, could be seen through binoculars. Parisian civilians fled south, while the French government escaped to Bordeaux.

The Germans too, with their supply lines impossibly stretched, were exhausted and underfed but, nonetheless, the Schlieffen Plan seemed to be going well. But then, Germany's commander-in-chief, Helmuth von Moltke, realising that Russia was mobilizing quicker than the plan anticipated, dispatched a portion of his fighting force to meet the threat from the east. Then, on the forty-first day of the war, on the River Marne, north of Paris, the now weakened Germans met a determined Allied resistance. The resultant Battle of the Marne (5–12 September) effectively ended Germany's attempt to capture Paris.

With Paris no longer a realistic objective, the

Germans headed north-west. The Allies, having so long been on the retreat, were now the pursuers, but, in their exhaustion, they pursued their enemy at a leisurely pace. The two sides next clashed at the inconclusive Battle of the Aisne. Having reached the elevated ground to the side of the River Aisne, fifty miles north of the River Marne, the Germans stopped and dug in. The Allies did likewise. The Germans extended their line of trenches northwards, swiftly followed by the Allies. And so it went on in what became known as the 'Race to the Sea'. Thus, by the end of October the zig-zag lines of trenches had reached the Channel coast, whilst, at the same time, the lines had extended southwards. Soon there was a line of opposing trenches, about 400 miles in length, running from the English Channel to the borders of Switzerland. The war of movement had come to an end.

Between October 1914 and the end of 1915, the Allies and the Germans had fought a number of inconclusive battles in the mire and mud of the Western Front.

Stalemate had ensued.

The Battle of Verdun

At the end of 1915, the new German commander-in-chief, Erich von Falkenhayn, decided that Germany's 'arch enemy' was not France, but Britain. But to destroy Britain's will Germany had first to defeat France. In a 'Christmas memorandum' to the German Kaiser, Falkenhayn proposed an offensive that would compel the French to 'throw in every man they have. If they do so,' he continued, 'the forces of France will bleed to death'. The place to do this, Falkenhayn declared, would be Verdun.

An ancient town in north-eastern France, Verdun was surrounded by a string of sixty interlocked and reinforced forts. On 21 February 1916, the Battle of Verdun began. 1,200 German guns lined over only eight miles pounded the city which, despite intelligence warning of the impending attack, remained poorly defended. Verdun, which held a symbolic tradition among the French, was deemed not so important by the upper echelon of France's military. Joseph Joffre, the French commander, was slow to respond until the exasperated French prime minister, Aristide Briand, paid a night-time visit. Waking Joffre from his slumber, Briand insisted that Joffre take the situation more seriously: 'You may not think losing Verdun a defeat – but everyone else will'.

Galvanised into action, Joffre dispatched his top general, Henri-Philippe Pétain, to organise a stern defence. Pétain managed to protect the only road leading into the city. Every day, while under continuous fire, 2,000 lorries made a return trip along the 45-mile *Voie Sacrée* ('Sacred Way') bringing in vital supplies and reinforcements to be fed into the furnace that had become Verdun. Serving under Pétain was General Robert Nivelle who famously promised that the Germans *on ne passe pas*, 'they shall not pass'.

Joseph Joffre, 1914.

The French were suffering grievous losses. Joffre demanded that his British counterpart, Sir Douglas Haig, open up the new offensive on the Somme, as previously agreed, to the north-west of Verdun, to take the pressure of his beleaguered men. Haig, concerned that his Kitchener recruits were not yet battle-ready, offered 15 August 1916 as a start date. In a lengthy dispatch, written on 23 December 1916, after the Battle of the Somme, Haig wrote that a 'very large proportion of the officers and men under my command were still far from being fully trained, and the longer the attack could be deferred the more efficient they would become'. When Haig tried this tact with Joffre, the Frenchman responded angrily that the French army would 'cease to exist' by mid-August. (In fact, Joffre was so angry, he had to be calmed down with 'liberal doses of 1840 brandy'.) Haig acquiesced and brought the offer forward to 25 June.

Joseph Joffre always refused to be told how many casualties his men had suffered, for it would only 'distract him' from his work. Following the heavy losses at Verdun, Joffre was replaced as c-in-c by Robert Nivelle in December 1916. As compensation, Joffre was awarded the ceremonious title of Marshal of France but from then on his role was restricted to a series of sinecure posts.

During June 1916, the attack and counterattack at Verdun continued. On the Eastern Front, the Russians fought the Austro-Hungarians, who, in turn, appealed to the Germans for help. Falkenhayn responded by calling a temporary halt at Verdun and transferring men east to aid the Austro-Hungarians.

The Battle of Verdun wound down, then fizzled out entirely, officially ending on 18 December 1916. Although the French, under the stewardship of Generals Pétain and Nivelle, had regained much of what they had lost after ten months of fighting, the city had been flattened. The Germans and French, between them, had lost up to 900,000 men – one death for every 90 seconds of the battle. Men on all sides were 'bled to death' but ultimately Falkenhayn's big push had achieved nothing.

The Somme Offensive: Plans and Preparations

And so we come back to the situation the British faced in the early summer of 1916 – the lack of experienced soldiers. But under pressure from the French, Haig and his team began preparations. They had no choice but to blood the inexperienced ranks of the 'Kitchener recruits'. Much of the burden of planning fell to Haig's number two, General Sir Henry Rawlinson, appointed commander of Britain's Fourth Army, the main force earmarked to spearhead Britain's Somme offensive. The responsibility must have weighed heavily upon their shoulders.

Beginning in early 1916, Haig and Rawlinson planned carefully and, much to Joffre's annoyance, slowly. The original wide-ranging objectives for the Somme, a breakthrough and deep penetration into German-held territory, were sized back. Now, as well as relieving French pressure at Verdun, the objective was to seize the railhead of Bapaume, about nine miles behind the German frontline. Bapaume, in the Nord-Pas-de-Calais region of northern France, had been occupied by the Germans since 26 September 1914.

The River Somme lies in the Picardy region of northern France. Ironically, given what was about to happen, the name Somme comes from a Celtic word meaning 'tranquillity'. In late 1914, the Germans and the French settled down to trench life without bothering each other too much. From August 1915 the British began to take over a sector north of the River Somme from the French Army. They were appalled to hear rumours that French and German officers would visit each other's quarters for a civilized drink or two and that enemy soldiers would swim in the river in full view of each other. But still, even with the more bellicose Brits, the area remained one of the quietest sectors on the whole Western Front.

Douglas Haig, c1913. Library of Congress.

With the coming offensive, civilians in the area were advised that if they wished to leave their homes they had to do so within 48 hours of the beginning of the bombardment and move only by daylight. If they opted to stay they had to provide themselves with enough food and provisions for ten days. After this, if they wished to leave they would not be permitted to use their vehicles or carts as the roads would be too busy with military transports.

The plan that Haig and Rawlinson initially devised was a wide fifteen to twenty-mile attack near the River Somme between the towns of Arras and Albert, comprising of 25 British infantry divisions and, to the south, nearer Albert, 40 French divisions. But with the French tied-up at Verdun, the number of French divisions was greatly reduced to six, and indeed the number of British infantry divisions was lowered to fourteen. As well as Bapaume, there were also a number of other towns Haig hoped to capture on the first day of hostilities – Mametz, Fricourt, La Boiselle, Thiepval and Beaumont Hamel, amongst others. (In the event, all but Bapaume were captured – but it took some four months, in some cases, not one day, to achieve). Haig envisioned a large, sweeping attack, an all-out offensive, going straight for the breakthrough; whereas Rawlinson preferred a 'bite and hold' advance – smaller, sequential steps.

(In January 1915, the statue of the Virgin Mary at

the top of the church in Albert was hit by a shell. The statue was knocked over and was left hanging precariously but it didn't fall. People began to say that when the statue fell, the war would end. It did fall – in April 1918. The war did end – but not for another seven months).

Statue of the Virgin Mary hanging from the Church of Notre Dame in Albert. Imperial War Museum.

The attack on the Somme would be preceded by a preliminary bombardment of the German lines,

4,500 yards in depth, utilizing some 1,500 artillery guns, about one big gun for every 17 yards of German frontline. Beginning on Saturday 24 June and lasting eight days, they would fire some 1.5 million shells (more than had been fired during the whole first year of the war). All of this happened as planned. The bombardment would utterly destroy all the German frontline defences and guns, including the barbed wire, and kill the German defenders or batter them so senseless to be unable to mount any form of counterattack. Once the shells had done their work, all the advancing troops had to do, so they were reliably informed, was to walk across No Man's Land and take possession of the German lines. Meanwhile, the French would make a subsidiary assault to guard and support the main British thrust. Amongst the French ranks were a few men from the Foreign Legion, including a number of Americans.

Yet, despite these grandiose plans, the British lacked the big guns and the high-explosive shells capable of inflicting any telling damage. The French, on the other hand, operating from a much shorter front, had double the number of big guns resulting in far fewer losses once the battle had started.

Haig, who as a younger man had served in the cavalry and, despite being a Scot, had represented England at polo, still believed that horses could play a vital role in an attack. The work of the infantry would be followed up by men on horses. With the German lines broken, his cavalry would be able to break through to the towns of Cambrai and Douai, breaking the German line in two.

That, at least, was the plan.

Naturally, the coming offensive was meant to be secret. But it wasn't. The poet-cum-soldier, Siegfried Sassoon, reckoned 'everyone at home' knew about it. Even his 'Aunt Evelyn was aware of the impending onslaught'.

The British prepared for the big day – 7,000 miles of telephone cable was laid and over 100 large water pipes providing fresh water put in place. Haig, in his December 1916 dispatch, summarized the preparations:

Vast stocks of ammunition and stores of all kinds had to be accumulated beforehand within a convenient distance of our front. To deal with these, many miles of new railways – both standard and narrow gauge – and trench tramways were laid. All available roads were improved, many others were made, and long causeways were built over marshy valleys.

Many additional dugouts had to be provided as shelter for the troops, for use as dressing stations for the wounded, and as magazines for storing ammunition, food, water, and engineering material. Scores of miles of deep communication trenches had to be dug, as well as trenches for telephone wires, assembly and assault trenches, and numerous gun emplacements and observation posts.

Many wells and borings were sunk, and over one hundred pumping plants were installed. More than one hundred and twenty miles of water mains were laid, and everything was got ready to ensure an adequate water supply as our troops advanced.

Much of this preparatory work had to be done under very trying conditions, and was liable to constant interruption from the enemy's fire.'

Indeed, the lack of 'roads' posed a problem. As one soldier later described it: 'No wheeled traffic can approach within three miles of the forward pits; for roads which were useful to the pre-war farmers have now disappeared. Everything must be carried up by men or mules'.

Originally, the battle was due to start on 25 June but this was put back to the 29th. Heavy rain and the realization that the bombardment hadn't yet been effective, forced it back a further two days. This was unfortunate for the men who had been moved up the line and were ready to go 'over the top', for it meant, having been kept at the front, they had to endure a miserable, soul-sapping 48 hours under continual rain.

So as planned, the preliminary bombardment, starting on 24 June and lasting night and day along a 12-mile front, was huge. An English journalist wrote, 'It seemed as though nothing could live, not an ant, under that stupendous artillery storm'. The noise of this bombardment was incredible. One British soldier described it as a 'continuous roar ... And it did not move'. A German Medical Officer, Lieutenant Stefan Westmann, wrote afterwards:

'For a full week we were under incessant bombardment. Day after day, the shells fell upon us. Our dugouts crumbled.

They'd fall on top of us and we'd have to dig ourselves and our comrades out. Sometimes we'd find them suffocated or smashed to pulp. Soldiers in bunkers came hysterical – they wanted to run out, and fights developed to keep them in the comparative safety of our deep bunkers. Even the rats became hysterical and came into our flimsy shelters to seek refuge from this terrific artillery fire. For seven days and seven nights we had nothing to eat and nothing to drink while shell after shell burst upon us.'

Instead of the usual 'fire and movement' advance, as infantrymen were trained to do, they were to walk across in upright and straight lines, one minute apart, laden with 70 pounds of equipment to secure the German frontline, ahead of the next advance to the second and then third lines. Once the infantrymen had crossed No Man's Land, they were not expecting to fight because the artillery would have done their work – the bombardment would have killed or cleared the Germans from their frontline trenches, so the equipment was needed to settle in and consolidate their newly-won gains. The provisions included their rifle, 150 rounds of ammunition, two hand grenades each, four empty sandbags, waterproof cape, steel helmet, a pair of goggles, field dressings, a spade, wire-cutters, a flare plus enough food and water for two days. Running would have been nigh-on impossible. 'We were reduced to the status of pack mules,' as one soldier later described it.

The evening before the start of the battle, Haig wrote in his diary, 'Preparations were never so thorough, nor troops better trained. Wire very well cut, and ammunition adequate... The weather report is favourable for tomorrow. With God's help, I feel hopeful'.

The Royal Flying Corps did their bit – flying sorties over the German lines to gain intelligence and destroy enemy observation balloons. Although, unfortunately, during the preliminary bombardment one RFC patrol returned and informed Haig what he hoped to hear – that the artillery had indeed done a good job of cutting the enemy wire. (The Royal Flying Corps would become the Royal Air Force, founded 1 April 1918).

The British would have preferred to have started the attack at 5.30 a.m. but the French claimed they needed the first two hours of light to complete their bombardment. Although the British were superior in numbers at the Somme, the French were considered more 'senior' and hence the time was set for 7.30 a.m.

The First Day, Saturday 1 July 1916

The rain of the preceding days had stopped; the weather was fine, the early morning mist lifting to reveal a clear blue sky. The final burst of artillery was the biggest yet – nearly a quarter of a million shells in little more than an hour, an average of 3,500 *every minute*. At 7.20 am, the first of nineteen mines that had been planted in tunnels beneath the German lines was detonated; a huge 40,000 pound explosion at Hawthorn Ridge, captured on moving film by official war photographer, Geoffrey Malins. The Hawthorn Crater is still visible today.

Explosion of the mine beneath Hawthorn Ridge, 7.20 am, 1 July 1916. Imperial War Museum.

Then, as the earth settled, an eerie silence prevailed. The massive explosions certainly alerted the German defenders of what was about to come – and they were ready. At precisely 7.30 a.m. whistles sounded up and down the British and French lines. The time had come.

Thus, laden with their provisions, the first of the 120,000 soldiers climbed the ladders out of the British trenches. The Battle of the Somme had started. (And lest we forget – most of these men were not professional soldiers; they were 'Kitchener recruits', in other words just two years previously they had been civilians, and, for the most part, had received only hurried and rudimentary training). Many sang as they walked towards their deaths; others recited the Lord's Prayer. To the right of the British, the smaller French force, transferred from the Battle of Verdun.

In order to squeeze through their own barbed wire, the troops bunched up, providing an easy target for the enemy guns. Those that got through advanced in rigid lines, as ordered, and were simply gunned down.

Infantrymen of the Tyneside Irish Brigade advancing across No Man's Land, 1 July, 1916. Imperial War Museum.

Captain Wilfred 'Billie' Nevill of the Royal East Surrey Regiment encouraged his men by giving each of his four platoons a football, each inscribed with the words 'European Cup'. The first platoon that kicked their football into a German trench would be declared the 'winner'. No one won. Within minutes, they were all shot down, including Captain Nevill.

Far from being decimated by the artillery, the German trenches ahead were brimming with guns pointing towards the advance. The bombardment had failed. But why? The Germans had occupied the area since 1914 and the chalky earth around the Somme was easy to dig, thus over the two years the Germans had been able to build a network of solid, well-constructed dugouts. Even the strongest of artillery guns, unless they scored a direct hit, was unlikely to cause these dugouts much damage. The dugouts further back from the frontline often had electricity, and, amazingly, panelled walls and plank floors. The German dugouts were indeed 'elaborate', as Haig described them: 'Sometimes in two storeys, and … connected up by passages as much as thirty feet below the surface of the ground (with) concrete machine gun emplacements. The front of the trenches in each system was protected by wire entanglements, many of them in two belts forty yards broad, built of iron stakes interlaced with barbed wire, often almost as thick as a man's finger'.

Interior of a German bunker, July 1916.
Imperial War Museum.

Later on during the war, shells would have had an impact as they were built with a fuse that would detonate on touching anything – even a thin shard of wire, but in 1916, the shells wouldn't detonate unless they fully hit the ground, therefore most merely pinged harmlessly off the wire entanglements. It didn't help that up to a third of the fired shells were duds and failed to detonate. (The lack of shells available to British artillery had caused a political scandal in May 1915. As a result, the production of shells increased but at the loss of quality, hence the artillery on the Somme was burdened with so many dud shells).

What followed went down as the worse day in British military history – 57,470 men fell on that first day alone, 19,240 of them dead. (If you add up the total number of British casualties at the Crimean, Boer and Korean Wars, they still wouldn't equal the number lost on this one day alone). Many of the wounded would subsequently die from their injuries. The French sustained 1,590 casualties. In return, the Germans suffered a 'mere' 8,000 casualties that first day. 500 Britons were taken prisoner. There were more casualties on this single day, 1 July 1916, than any other day of the war. The Newfoundland Regiment (later the *Royal* Newfoundland Regiment), for example, sustained 90 per cent casualties – of the 780 Newfoundlanders that advanced on 1 July, only

74 were available for duty the following day. The Accrington Pals also suffered terribly. It was their first time in battle. Of about 700 that went over, 235 were killed and 350 wounded – in the first twenty minutes. Most of them hadn't even had chance to fire a single bullet. As one veteran later said, '(We were) two years in the making, ten minutes in the destroying'.

Royal Irish Riflemen, July 1916. Imperial War Museum.

Successive lines of advancing troops had to step over the many men lying dead or wounded. Young officers carried little more than a pistol and a walking stick. Soon, the ground in front and around the British frontline became so clogged-up, that men had to start their advance from the second line. Many didn't even make it as far as their own frontline before they were shot down. Thus, most of the dead lay on British territory.

One British general heaped praise on the men as they 'advanced in line after line, dressed as if on parade, and not a man shirked going through the extremely heavy barrage, or facing the machine-gun and rifle fire that finally wiped them out. Yet not a man wavered, broke the ranks, or attempted to come back. I have never seen, I would never have imagined, such a magnificent display of gallantry, discipline and determination'. Another British general at the Battle of the Somme, Sir Beauvoir de Lisle, wrote, 'It was a remarkable display of training and discipline, and the attack failed only because dead men cannot move on'.

The Scottish novelist, John Buchan, author of *The Thirty-Nine Steps*, described the 'splendid troops (shedding) their blood like water for the liberty of the world'.

Those few who did make it as far as the German

frontline (and not many of those came back) were appalled to find the German barbed wire hadn't been cut in any way whatsoever. One infantryman described the wire as 'so dense that daylight could barely be seen through it. Through the glasses it looked a black mass. The German faith in massed wire had paid off'. At one point on the first day, German stretcher-bearers emerged under a white flag to rescue wounded British near their wire.

British Soldiers of the Cheshire Regiment, near Albert, July 1916. Imperial War Museum.

Communication, or the lack of it, exacerbated the situation. The trenches for telephone wires that Haig described in his dispatch were destroyed by German counter artillery bombardment. To be safe from damage, the lines should have been buried at a depth of 1.5 feet but for the engineers working under fire this was utterly impractical. Beyond sending a runner to and fro with written messages, communication between officers behind the lines and the men in battle was difficult. And runners, liable to get shot or lost in the heat of battle, are notoriously an unreliable method of relaying messages.

The day did return some success – especially for the French in the southern sector. The French, operating from a much narrower sector than the British, were better able to concentrate their artillery fire, and the German lines opposite them were not so heavily defended. Hence, the French were able to seize a mile of German territory and captured some 4,000 Germans. But, with the French lacking reinforcements, the Germans were able to regain much of the lost ground. At no point on 1 July did either the French or the British penetrate the second

German line. But the clash at the Somme did alleviate the pressure felt by the French at Verdun, as the German commanders immediately transferred troops from one to the other.

Britain's Royal Army Medical Corps (RAMC) was ready – to a degree. There were 15 casualty clearing stations (CCSs) behind the British lines at the Somme, each one, in effect, a mini-hospital consisting of operating theatres, x-ray machines and wards able to accommodate 1,500 beds. They were staffed with extra nurses and, between them, 174 medical officers. Field ambulances and specialist teams waited on hand; ready to move wherever they were needed.

A wounded soldier would first be treated at Regimental Aid Post situated in a trench just behind the front line. Having quickly been assessed and had a dressing clapped on, he'd be sent back, sometimes on foot if the man was capable of it, to an Advance Dressing Station a couple miles behind the front. From there, assuming he wasn't fit enough to return to the front, he would be evacuated to the next point of treatment, the Casualty Clearing Station.

*Wounded British troops wearing German helmets outside a Casualty Clearing Station, September 1916.
Imperial War Museum.*

It was assumed that 15 CCSs would be enough. It wasn't. Inundated with casualties within the first hour, it soon became apparent that this was hugely insufficient. The men and women medics worked round the clock as numbers built up. Wounded men in their hundreds had to lie on stretchers in tents or marquees untreated for hours, or days. Soon the tents and stretchers were all used up, leaving many to lie on the bare ground outside. Fortunately, the weather in early July remained fine, and the nights were not too cold. Men with shell fragments or bits of metal embedded in them need immediate attention to prevent the onslaught of sepsis. Yet, with only the most serious cases being attended to straightaway, they had no choice but to wait. Thus many who could have been saved died simply from the lack of being seen and treated in time.

Between them, the 15 CCSs treated about 45,000 wounded within the first week of fighting at the Somme.

MO's carried out amputation after amputation for hours at a time. Second opinions were not sought. Alerted by the tell-tale stench, the main thing was to prevent the spread of gas gangrene. Burial parties worked non-stop. 400 RAMC doctors were killed or wounded during the Battle of the Somme.

From the CCS, the wounded would be put on ambulance trains or barges and sent back to a hospital on a base – towns like Le Havre on the Channel coast. The trains ran round the clock – depositing men at the base and returning to the CCSs for the next contingent. From there, again, assuming they were not fit enough to return to the front, they would be transported back across the Channel and transferred to a hospital somewhere in Britain. The problem however was the sheer numbers of men waiting evacuation. With so many wounded, many had to make the journey without having been seen or even cleaned up, and so had to make do in their mud and blood-caked uniforms and filthy dressings crudely applied on the field. Infection was rife.

*A RAMC ambulance barge, August 1916.
Imperial War Museum.*

People in Britain, seeing the huge numbers of ragged and wounded men returning home, were shocked. The newspapers had talked of success but the mere sight of these men told a different story. Listening to their tales confirmed the worse.

Hospitals across the country were equally inundated. Typically, three men would have to share two beds pushed together, sometimes with another couple of men on stretchers balanced above them on the bed rails. The backrooms soon became full – a billiards table, for example, could accommodate a number of wounded men. Even back in Britain, men with lighter wounds would still have to wait days to been seen, which meant at the very point the army urgently needed reinforcements, these potentially fit men were still laid up in a hospital.

Many of the wounded staggered back from the battle with physical paralysis, severe twitching or shaking, temporary blindness or deafness, and amnesia. They were suffering from what was dismissively called 'shell shock'. When one MO declared a group of 100 soldiers as unfit for further service because of shell shock, he was censured for displaying 'undue sympathy with the men'. The British Army simply did not understand shell shock at this stage. The term was a disingenuous term for malingering. Indeed, from early 1917, the army banned the RAMC from using the phrase.

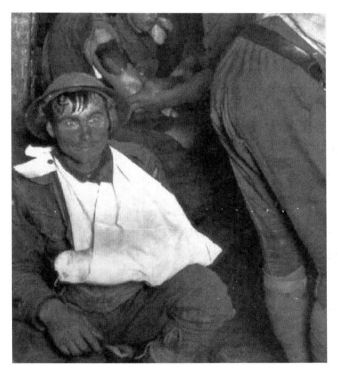

Wounded Australian soldier with the 'thousand-yard stare', a common symptom of shell shock.

Although the number of 'successes' on 1 July was limited, one wouldn't have thought so from reading a statement issued by the British Army based in Paris:

The first day of the offensive is very satisfactory. The success is not a thunderbolt, as has happened earlier in similar operations, but it is important above all because it is rich in promises. It is no longer a question here of attempts to pierce as with a knife. It is rather a slow, continuous, and methodical push, sparing in lives, until the day when the enemy's resistance, incessantly hammered at, will crumple up at some point. From today the first results of the new tactics permit one to await developments with confidence.'

The newspapers were also full of optimism, reporting that 'British troops have already occupied the German frontline'.

John Buchan also thought the day had been a success: 'The attack failed nowhere … by the afternoon all our tasks had been accomplished. The audacious enterprise had been crowned with unparalleled success. Germans may write on their badges that God is with them, but our lads – they know'.

Many journalists were appalled when they realised that, contrary to what they had been told, the attack on that first day had not be an overwhelming success. One reporter for the *Daily Mail* later wrote, 'A great part of the information supplied to us by (British Army Intelligence) was utterly wrong and misleading. The dispatches were largely untrue so far as they deal with concrete results. For myself, on the next day and yet more on the day after that, I was thoroughly and deeply ashamed of what I had written, for the very good reason that it was untrue. Almost all the official information was wrong'.

Despite the grievous losses on the first day and the failure to reinstate a war of movement, Douglas Haig wrote that 'the enemy has undoubtedly been severely shaken and he has few reserves in hand. Our correct course, therefore, is to press him hard with the least possible delay'. On visiting a casualty clearing station, he found the men to be in 'wonderful good spirits'. Joseph Joffre remained determined that there should be no let-up in the British offensive. The survival of the French army at Verdun depended on it. Thus the attack was resumed the following day. And the day after that.

A German prisoner helps British wounded, Bazentin Ridge, 19 July 1916. Imperial War Museum.

2 July – 18 November 1916

Within the overriding 'Battle of the Somme', there were a number of integrated battles and engagements:

Battle of Albert, 1–13 July
Battle of Bazentin Ridge, 14–17 July
Battle of Delville Wood, 14 July–15 September
Battle of Fromelles, 19–20 July
Battle of Pozières Ridge, 23 July–7 August
Battle of Guillemont, 3–6 September
Battle of Ginchy, 9 September
Battle of Flers–Courcelette, 15–22 September
Battle of Morval, 25–28 September
Battle of Thiepval Ridge, 26–28 September
Battle of the Transloy Ridges, 1 October–11 November

Battle of the Ancre Heights, 1 October–11 November
Battle of the Ancre, 13–18 November.

Men advancing in the days that followed found many of their dead and dying colleagues from the preceding days. Some, as one officer described it, had 'crawled into a shell-hole, wrapped their waterproofs around them, taken their bibles out and died like that'. Siegfried Sassoon went over the top on 4 July. In his diary, he described a scene:

'These dead are terrible and undignified carcasses, stiff and contorted. There were thirty of our own laid in two ranks by the Mametz Carnoy road, some side by side on their backs with clotted fingers mingled as if they were handshaking in the companionship of death. And the stench undefinable. And rags and shreds of blood-stained cloth, bloody boots riddled and torn'.

Burying the dead proved utterly impractical. One Australian wrote, 'We had neither time nor space for burials, and the wounded could not be got away. They stayed with us and died, pitifully, with us, and then they rotted. The stench of the battlefield spread for miles around. And the sight of the limbs, the mangled bodies, and stray heads... we lived with all this for eleven days'.

The Road to Pozières, August 1916.
Australian War Museum.

As July wore on, there were more minor successes in the southern sector of the battle, but nothing much in the north. The battle for the Pozières Ridge, for example, was won following a determined Australian attack (the first time

Australians had fought on the Western Front) but at a high cost – 23,000 Australians were killed or wounded in just two week of fighting – compared to the 28,150 casualties during the eight-month Gallipoli campaign (April 1915 – January 1916). As one Australian historian described it, Pozières Ridge is 'more densely sown with Australian sacrifice than any other place on earth'.

The Battle of Delville Wood, which started on 14 July, was a similar story – a successful assault but one that cost dearly – of the 3,153 South Africans that went into battle at Delville Wood, only 773 returned unscathed. But the Germans, exhausted and running out of ammunition, surrendered in large numbers.

On 14 July, following a partially successful night-time attack, the British sent in the cavalry – a rare sight on the Western Front of the First World War and one that stirred the romantic notions in old-timers such as Haig. But the horses became bogged down in the mud, the Germans opened fire and few survived, either horse or man.

From late July, the British started using 'creeping barrage', a new concept of protecting advancing infantry with a 'curtain' of artillery fire fifty or so yards in front of them. The barrage would 'creep' forward at the same pace as the men, providing continued protection. Thus shielded, the attackers would seize the German frontline, and then advance to capture the second and third lines. But it invariably failed to work. Based on a pre-arranged timetable, the artillery, men who were as inexperienced in their job as the infantry was in theirs, often lost track and invariably ended-up running out of sync with the advancing infantry. It meant the British soldier stepping across No Man's Land was either without the protection of the barrage that was aimed too far ahead of him or too far behind or, worse, shelled by his own artillery. The lack of immediate communication meant it took an age for the situation to be rectified.

Held by the Germans, the town of Guillemont separated the British and French forces. By holding it, the Germans were able to prevent the Allies from operating in unison. Despite earlier costly failures, the British were determined to capture it. Again, after a series of attacks and counter-attacks, the cost, on all sides, was appallingly high. On 6 September, after three days of intense fighting, Guillemont finally fell to the British. One British doctor, walking through Guillemont shortly after the battle, wrote, 'As I walked along the sunken road that ran through the middle of the village; it is not much exaggeration to say that one could have walked the length of the village stepping from corpse to corpse without putting a foot on the ground'. From Guillemont, the British were able to capture the village of Ginchy.

British soldiers with a Vickers machine gun, July 1916.

The Germans were under strict instruction that

they had to regain every yard of lost ground, whether it was of tactical value or not, a policy of no retreat. Thus, German losses soon mounted, equalling and even surpassing Allied casualties. It was turning into a battle with no winners. The Germans lost some 135,000 men during the month of September, their worst month of the battle, forcing them to withdraw a mile back. Yet, the ultimate breakthrough that Haig was aiming for remained elusive.

Working under terrifically dangerous conditions and with bulky equipment, filmmaker Geoffrey Malins, and his assistant cameraman, John McDowell, filmed several scenes from the battle (although many were staged or re-enacted). They were lucky to be there – Haig hated and distrusted all forms of press and media. One memorable scene captures a group of soldiers playing up for the camera, minutes before they were due to go into battle. Half of them would be dead within thirty minutes.

The resultant 77-minute film, *The Battle of the Somme*, having passed both military and political scrutiny, was shown in cinemas throughout the UK from August 1916. David Lloyd George, at the time

Britain's War Secretary, urged the public to go and see it: 'I am convinced,' he said, 'that when you have seen this wonderful picture every heart will beat in sympathy with its purpose ... Herald the deeds of our brave men to the ends of the earth. This is your duty!' Within six weeks, some 20 million Britons (half the population) had seen the film. It was, for most, a cathartic experience – here they were watching on film the reality of war that few had imagined, or dared to imagine. In truth, many of the worst scenes had been cut. Although the authorities had wanted the British public to appreciate the efforts their men were making on their behalf, they also wanted to emphasise that their efforts were for the good. As Malins himself said in his 1920 memoir, *How I Filmed the War*:

'You must not leave the public with a bitter taste in their mouth at the end. The film takes you to the grave, but it must not leave you there; it shows you death in all its grim nakedness; but after that it is essential that you should be restored to a sense of cheerfulness and joy. That joy comes of the knowledge that in all this whirlpool of horrors our lads continue to smile the smile of victory'.

Scene from Geoffrey Malins' film, The Battle of the Somme. *The wounded man died 30 minutes after reaching the trenches. Imperial War Museum.*

A German film, *With Our Heroes on the Somme*, came out at the same time but filled with many obviously faked scenes, it was never a success.

In mid-August, King George V spent five days visiting the battlefield.. In a statement issued after returning to London, the king wrote:

Do not think that I and your fellow-countrymen forget the heavy sacrifices which the Armies have made and the bravery and endurance they have displayed during the past two years of bitter conflict. These sacrifices have not been in vain; the arms of the Allies will never be laid down until our cause has triumphed. I return home more than ever proud of you'.

King George V and the Prince of Wales inspect captured German trenches near Fricourt with General Sir Henry Rawlinson et al, *14 August 1916. Imperial War Museum.*

On 15 September, Haig introduced the modern equivalent of the cavalry onto the battlefield – the 'landship'. Originated in Britain, and championed by Winston Churchill, at the time the First Lord of the Admiralty, the designers tried to disguise them as water storage 'tanks'. The name stuck. Despite advice to wait for more testing, Haig insisted on their use at the Somme. In fact, he had hoped they'd be ready to use on the first day. Finally he got his way and the introduction of 36 'Mark 1' thirty ton tanks with a top speed of 3.7 miles per hour met with mixed results – many broke down but a few managed to penetrate German lines 'frightening the Jerries out of their wits and making them scuttle like frightened rabbits', as one witness described it. With the intense noise of the engine and the exhaust fumes, it was probably just as frightening for the men inside. The eight-man crew was issued with chainmail face visors and they knew that although safe from most shell explosions, a direct hit could incinerate them.

As always, the Germans soon plugged the hole forged by the tanks. Nonetheless, Haig was impressed and immediately ordered a thousand more. One English witness described three of these 'huge mechanical monsters' accidentally firing on its own trench: 'Giving no thought to his own personal safety as he saw the tanks firing on his own men, the colonel ran forward and furiously rained blows with his cane on the side of one of the tanks'. Another described a fallen comrade run over by one of these 'land crabs', as he called them: 'This body was just a splash of blood and clothing about two feet wide and perhaps an inch thick. An hour before this thing had been a thinking breathing man, with life before him and loved ones awaiting him probably somewhere in Scotland, for he was a kiltie'.

British Mark I tank, near Thiepval, 25 September 1916. Imperial War Museum.

Tanks were an integral part of the assault involving Canadian and New Zealand troops on the

German-held village of Flers, 15-22 September. The Allies managed to push their frontline forward by 2,500–3,000 yards and caused severe casualties on the German defenders.

In September, the British used poison gas and tanks when attacking the Germans at Thiepval Ridge. (Gas had first been successfully used by the Germans on the first day of the Second Battle of Ypres on 22 April 1915 when 168 tons of chlorine gas caused some 6,000 casualties amongst French-colonial troops. There had been an unsuccessful attempt on the Eastern Front the previous year but the gas froze in mid-air. This new terrible weapon was inhumane, cried the Allied generals, only to be using it themselves within five months at the Battle of Loos). On 26 September 1916, British and Canadian troops successfully forced the Germans from the village of Thiepval.

The future prime minister, Harold Macmillan, saw action at the Somme. On 15 September, the day the tanks first went into action, he was badly wounded and lay in a trench for over ten hours, feigning death when any Germans passed, reading

Aeschylus in the original Greek before taking a dose of morphine and falling asleep. He was eventually rescued by a sergeant who asked him, 'Thank you, sir, for leave to carry you away'. The injuries Macmillan sustained that day remained with him and caused him to walk with a shuffle for the rest of his life.

The prime minister up to December 1916 was Herbert Asquith. His son, Raymond, was a fellow officer in Harold Macmillan's regiment. Raymond was also wounded on 15 September. He lay on a stretcher, calmly lit a cigarette and died shortly afterwards. Raymond's death hit Herbert Asquith hard, leaving him feeling emotionally 'bankrupt'.

Another 'celebrity' to fight at the Somme was the mountaineer, George Mallory. A second lieutenant, he fought under Gwilym Lloyd George, the son of the next prime minister, David Lloyd George. In a letter to his parents, Mallory described the trenches as being 'as harrowing as you can imagine when one sees the dead and dying'. In another letter, this one to his wife, he wrote, 'I don't object to corpses so long as they are fresh ... With the wounded it is different. It always distresses me to see them'.

George Mallory, c1915.

(Mallory and a climbing partner disappeared on Mount Everest in June 1924 whilst attempting the first ascent of the world's highest mountain. His body was not found until 1999. No one knows for sure whether they died on the ascent or descent).

The first black officer in the British Army, Walter Tull, also fought at the Somme. A professional footballer who, pre-war, had played for Tottenham Hotspurs and Northampton Town (the first black outfield player), he joined the Footballers' Battalion of the Middlesex Regiment. He was commissioned as an officer in 1917 despite a military law that forbade men not 'of pure European descent' from becoming officers. He fought on the Italian Front, was recommended for a Military Cross, returned to France and was killed in action on 25 March 1918.

Walter Tull, c1916.

Vera Brittain's brother, Edward, also a second lieutenant, saw action on 1 July. He was wounded in the left arm and the right thigh and subsequently won a Military Cross for his actions at the Somme. Edward was evacuated back to England to a hospital in Camberwell in London where, by sheer coincidence, he was treated by his sister who was working there as a Voluntary Aid Detachment (VAD) nurse. Edward Brittain recovered from his wounds and later returned to action. He was killed in action also on the Italian Front on 15 June 1918.

John Ronald Reuel Tolkien, who would achieve fame for his *Lord of the Rings* trilogy, had been at the Somme for three months when he came down with 'trench fever', a disease carried by lice, and had to be invalided back home where he spent a month in hospital in Birmingham. After the war, he wrote, 'One has indeed personally to come under the shadow of war to feel fully its oppression ... By 1918 all but one of my close friends were dead'.

The author of *I, Claudius* and *Goodbye to All That*, Robert Graves, serving as a captain in the Royal Welch (*sic*) Fusiliers, was so badly wounded by a shell burst at High Wood that he was about to be buried. It was only at the point of burial that someone noticed

Graves was still breathing. His parents were informed of his supposed death, and *The Times* printed his obituary. A week later, they were obliged to publish an addendum: 'Captain Robert Graves, Royal Welch Fusiliers, officially reported died of wounds, wishes to inform his friends that he is recovering from his wounds at Queen Alexandra's Hospital, Highgate'. Having returned home, Graves recovered and was able to resume his military duties. Later in the war, he was hospitalized with shell-shock.

Actor Arnold Ridley ('Godfrey' in Dad's Army) suffered terrible injuries during the First World War and was left psychologically scarred for the rest of his life. He had volunteered in 1914 but was rejected on account of a broken toe sustained while playing rugby. Accepted two years later, he fought at the Somme. During the Battle of Delville Wood, Ridley's battalion experienced nearly 50 per cent casualties. He later pointed out: 'It wasn't a question of "if I get killed", it was merely a question of "when I get killed"'. A German bayonet cut the tendons to his left-hand fingers. Hoping for a 'Blighty', a wound serious enough to have you invalided home but not life-threatening or life-changing, Ridley was disappointed not to have lost his hand. It was not, he later said, 'a right thought for a young man to hope he's been maimed for life'. His skull was cracked by a German rifle butt and he suffered a bayonet wound to his groin. He had nightmares for the rest of his life. Conditions in the trenches left him with feet 'twisted like a tramp's' and, according to his son, 'he lost all his teeth... the use of three fingers in his left hand, and had shrapnel coming out of his back for years'.

On 17 September, Manfred von Richthofen, the German 'Red Baron' (so called for painting his aircraft red), claimed his first 'confirmed' kill over the Somme battlefield. He described the encounter in detail. 'My Englishman twisted and turned, flying in zigzags.' Eventually, von Richthofen shot the English plane down, killing the observer, Tom Rees, and wounding its pilot. Later, he said, 'I honoured the fallen enemy (Rees) by placing a stone on his beautiful grave'. Von Richthofen claimed 80 kills before he was brought down himself and killed on 21 April 1918.

Adolf Hitler, deployed as a runner, served at the Somme, describing it in his semi-autobiographical work, *Mein Kampf* ('My Struggle'), as 'more like hell than war'. On 7 October, Hitler was wounded in the left thigh when a shell exploded at the entrance of his dugout. He begged not to be evacuated but his injuries were serious enough to warrant four months in a hospital at Beelitz in north-west Germany.

Adolf Hitler, far left, c1914.
National Archives and Records Administration.

Returning back home to Germany after two years at the front, Hitler wrote, 'I could scarcely imagine how Germans looked when not in uniform'. Once recovered, he requested an immediate return to the frontline. His wish was granted in March 1917.

Arthur Conan Doyle's son, Kingsley, was wounded in the neck on the first day of the Somme. Two years later, however, Kingsley was recovering. But in the summer of 1918, the whole world was swept by 'Spanish Flu', the most devastating pandemic in modern times which claimed at least 50 million lives. Among them, on 28 October, was 25-year-old Kingsley, his resistance compromised by his battlefield injury.

Arthur Conan Doyle was a leading proponent for spiritualism. His greatest invention, the straight-laced Sherlock Holmes, would have thoroughly disapproved of his creator's conversion to séances, Ouija boards and mediums. Conan Doyle once professed, 'After weighing the evidence, I could no more doubt the existence of [life on the other side] than I could doubt the existence of lions in Africa'. On another occasion, he declared, 'Christianity is dead. How else could ten million young men have marched out to slaughter? Did any moral force stop that war? No. Christianity is dead!' Like so many grief-struck parents, Conan Doyle was desperate to commune with his dead son from beyond the grave. In his memoirs, he describes 'talking' to Kingsley. 'Are you happy?' he asks him. 'Yes, I am so happy,' comes the reply.

Other famous people who served on the Somme included playwright J B Priestley; German Expressionist artist Otto Dix; Hugh Dowding, leader of RAF Fighter Command during the Battles of France and Britain; and Antony Eden, another future British prime minister. Those that died at the Somme included the composer George Butterworth. In mid-July, he was awarded the Military Cross but, being killed on 5 August, did not live to receive it. His name is amongst those listed as missing on the Thiepval Memorial.

The oldest British soldier to die during the First World War was killed at the Somme. Aged 67, his name was Henry Webber. Despite being far too old for active service and rejected several times, he somehow managed to join up, serving as a lieutenant in the South Lancashire Regiment. His three sons were all serving as officers and apparently he had been motivated by their stoic efforts. He joked that if he happen to meet any of his sons, he would have to salute them. On 27 July, near Mametz Wood, Webber was killed by a shell. His wife received a message of sympathy from the King and the Army – most unusual for a lieutenant but probably because of his age. Webber's commanding officer wrote, 'He was so gallant and full of energy. We all had the greatest admiration and respect for him'. His three sons all survived the war.

On 20 July, 19-year-old Private John Bennett of the Hampshire Regiment was sentenced to two years' imprisonment with hard labour for having gone absent without leave. Less than three weeks later, on 8 August, the Germans launched a gas attack. Bennett, who was serving under a suspended sentence, fled the trenches. When he returned, he found that six of his comrades had been killed in the gas attack, and a further 46 wounded. He was arrested and tried under the charge of 'misbehaving before the enemy in such a manner as to show cowardice'. Refusing to be represented, he was found guilty. Between August 1914 and October 1918 there were around 238,000 courts martial, of which 3,080 resulted in the death sentence. Of these, 346 (11 per cent) were carried out – 40 for murder, the other 306 for offences such as desertion, cowardice, falling asleep while on duty, *etc*. (In November 2006, the UK government pardoned the 306). No execution could take place until it had been confirmed by the commander-in-chief (John French or, from December 1915, Douglas Haig). So, in 89 per cent of cases, the c-in-c commuted the sentence to imprisonment or hard labour. Unfortunately for Bennett, he was one of the 11 per cent – Douglas Haig signed the papers of authorization and John Bennett was executed on 28 August.

Another private charged and executed for the same offence was Harry Farr of the West Yorkshire Regiment. Farr was arrested after refusing to go to the trenches. He'd asked to return to base camp, saying he could not stand the noise of artillery and was not in a fit state. Following a 20-minute court martial on 17 October 1916, 25-year-old Farr was found guilty. He was shot the following morning. At his execution, he refused a blindfold, preferring, he said, to look the firing squad straight in the eye. The army chaplain at the execution wrote Farr's widow a letter saying 'a finer soldier never lived'.

Three British officers were executed during the war – the first, Lieutenant Eric Skeffington Poole, during the Battle of the Somme. Born in Nova Scotia, his family moved to England in the 1900s and Poole joined the British Army in 1914 and the following year was commissioned as an officer. According to his medical record, on 7 July 1916, having been hit by clods of earth and partially buried by a heavy bout of German shelling, he suffered shell shock and perhaps a degree of brain damage. After a few weeks off, he returned to duty in August. On 5 October, during the Battle of Flers, he got confused and wandered away from the platoon he was commanding and disappeared for a couple of days. On being found, he was arrested and put on trial for desertion while 'on active service'. Poole admitted that since the incident in July, he got easily confused and had 'great difficulty in making up [his] mind'.

A Royal Army Medical Corps officer, speaking in Poole's defence, told the trial that given Poole's condition, he was incapable of intentionally deserting.

But a medical report disagreed, concluding that Poole was 'of sound mind and capable of appreciating the nature and quality of his actions'. He was found guilty of desertion and condemned to death. Haig confirmed the sentence and, in his diary, wrote, 'such a crime is more serious in the case of an officer than of a man and also it is highly important that all ranks should realise the law is the same for an officer as a private'. Aged 31, Eric Skeffington Poole was executed by firing squad on 10 December 1916.

Eric Skeffington Poole

51 Victoria Crosses were awarded during the Battle of the Somme, 17 posthumously; nine were awarded on the first day alone, six posthumously. The first was posthumously awarded to Irishman, 20-year-old William 'Billy' McFadzean. Hours before the attack on the 1 July, McFadzean, a keen rugby player, and his comrades were carrying boxes of grenades down a communication trench. McFadzean's box burst open, the six grenades fell and two pins slipped from their grenades. Knowing they had only seconds before the grenades detonated, McFadzean selflessly threw himself on top of them, thus absorbing the impact, and, in the process, was blown to pieces. The citation, published in the *London Gazette*, stated, 'without a moment's hesitation [McFadzean] gave his life for his comrades'.

Only three men have been awarded the Victoria Cross twice. One of them, Noel Chavasse, a medical doctor and stretcher-bearer for the Royal Army Medical Corps, received his first at the Somme. In his younger day, Noel and his twin brother, Christopher, had both competed in the 400 metres at the 1908 London Olympics, although neither won a medal.

Noel Chavasse, c1916.

Noel Chavasse won his first VC on 9 August 1916. The citation stated that 'During an attack he tended the wounded in the open all day, under heavy fire, frequently in view of the enemy. During the ensuing night he searched for wounded on the ground in front of the enemy's lines for four hours'. He continued his work the following day and night. The citation finishes: 'Altogether he saved the lives of some twenty badly wounded men, besides the ordinary cases which passed through his hands. His courage and self-sacrifice, were beyond praise'. Chavasse won his second VC at Passchendaele at the beginning of August 1917 but died of his wounds a few days later, aged 32.

Conditions in the trenches, both Allied and German, were foul. Mud everywhere, decaying corpses, putrid water, filth, flies, rats and lice made for a horrible and grim environment. October gave way to November, and with November came the rain, the cold and snow. The terrain, already clogged-up, became a quagmire, making it almost impossible to move supplies and equipment around. After 141 days of fighting, the battle finally terminated on 18 November.

The Battle is Over

Technically, the Battle of the Somme may be considered an Allied victory but it was perhaps a 'Pyrrhic Victory'. The British and Commonwealth forces suffered 419,654 dead, wounded and missing (an average of almost 3,000 men *every single day*); the French 204,253 and the Germans an estimated 650,000. (Between Verdun and the Somme, the Germans sustained a million casualties). For this the Allies had gained five miles. The original objective of capturing the German-held village of Bapaume had failed. The Allies only managed to recapture the village on 17 March 1917, and on 24 March 1918, the

Germans took the village back again. But the battle did succeed in relieving the French at the Battle of Verdun – which came to an end on 21 December 1916. So in that sense the Battle of the Somme was a success.

*Beaumont Hamel, November 1916.
Imperial War Museum.*

The Somme Offensive certainly affected British morale both of the fighting soldier and domestically, back in Britain. Enthusiasm for the war had already been in decline and the number of young men coming through to sign-up fell drastically. One British private wrote that after the Somme, many 'veterans, myself included, decided to do no more than was necessary – following orders but, if possible, keeping out of harm's way'.

In March 1916, the British government had introduced conscription for all single men aged between 18 and 41. The medically unfit, farmers, miners, clergymen, teachers and certain industrial workers, such as munition workers, were deemed exempt, as well as conscientious objectors, although many 'conchies' were given civilian jobs or non-fighting roles at the front, such as stretcher-bearers. A second act passed in May 1916 extended conscription to married men. Conscription did not include Ireland, even though it was still part of the United Kingdom. In 1918, the upper age limit was raised to 51.

In early 1917, post-Somme, the Germans, knowing they could not afford to lose any more men holding the frontline, pulled their forces back to the heavily-fortified second line, the Hindenburg Line. And so we have the greatest irony of the Battle of the

Somme – within months the Germans voluntarily abandoned the land they fought so hard to maintain between July and November 1916, allowing the British to occupy the very soil that had seen some 420,000 of their men perish. Erich von Falkenhayn had wanted to see the French 'bled dry' at Verdun. In the event, all sides on the Western Front had suffered. Yet the war, as we know, still had two years to go.

There is the case to be made that, in the long term, the Battle of the Somme helped defeat the Germans. One member of the German General Staff wrote that the Somme was the 'muddy grave of the German field army'. Falkenhayn had still been in charge at the Somme until August when he was sacked and replaced by Generals Paul von Hindenburg, aged 69, and Erich Ludendorff, two men who had previously found military fame on the Eastern Front. Ludendorff declared that the German army was 'exhausted' following the Somme.

Knowing now that Germany could not defeat the Allies on the Western Front, Ludendorff hoped to starve Britain into submission by sinking ships bringing supplies and food to Great Britain, whether the ships were British or neutral. This policy of 'unrestricted submarine warfare' resulted in a large number of American ships being sunk, and other ships with US citizens aboard. The most infamous occasion being the sinking of the British ocean liner, the RMS *Lusitania*, on 7 May 1915. Amongst the 1,198 victims were 128 American civilians.

Paul von Hindenburg and Erich Ludendorff, September 1916. German Federal Archives.

Two years later, on 6 April 1917, the US declared war on Germany. The Allies were delighted – the US with its huge resources of manpower and material output would surely make all the difference. It did. The first 14,000 American troops landed on French soil on 26 June 1917. At this stage they were still untrained, unprepared and ill-equipped. But with time that changed, and the arrival of fresh troops, 10,000 a day by September 1918, greatly boosted morale and almost guaranteed Germany's defeat.

In 1917, the Russian Revolution brought some respite for the Germans. On 15 March, the Russian tsar, Nicholas II, was forced to abdicate, bringing to an end the 300-year-old Romanov dynasty. (He was later executed). Yet, Russia remained committed to the war. It wasn't until the Bolsheviks, led by Vladimir Lenin, seized power in November did Russia finally lay down its arms. On 3 March 1918, Russia signed a humiliating surrender, the Treaty of Brest-Litovsk. The Eastern Front had come to an end. Germany, therefore, was able to transfer huge numbers of men and equipment from the Eastern to the Western Front.

But by then, the numerical advantage had been nullified by the arrival of the Americans.

US soldier with a captured German prisoner, Battle of St. Quentin Canal, 29 September 1918.

Haig almost lost his job as a result of the Somme. He was certainly disliked by David Lloyd George, prime minister from 6 December 1916 (to October 1922), who called him a 'dunce'. In his memories, Lloyd George wrote, 'I never met a man in a high position who seemed to me so utterly devoid of imagination', calling him a man of 'sound intelligence of secondary quality'. But Haig had the confidence of the British establishment and, importantly, King George V, and hence survived. Indeed, at Passchendaele (July to November 1917), Haig launched another frontal assault as deadly and ultimately as fruitless as the Somme. But he was also in charge of British forces during the Allies' 'Hundred Day Offensive', 8 August to 11 November 1918, a series of battles which steadily pushed the Germans beyond the Hindenburg Line, out of France, and ultimately led to victory.

With Haig's 'Hundred Day Offensive' proving a success, the Germans, exhausted both at home and on the battlefield, agreed to sign an armistice. On 8 November 1918, a German delegation headed by Matthias Erzberger met the French, headed by Ferdinand Foch, in a railway carriage in the woods of Compiègne, north of Paris. Erzberger and his team had come to seek an armistice; Foch to dictate its terms. Signed at 5 a.m, French time, on 11 November, the Western Front Armistice came into effect six hours later at 11 a.m – 'the eleventh hour of the eleventh day of the eleventh month'.

The First World War was over.

*German soldier at the Battle of the Somme, 1916.
German Federal Archives.*

Postscript

The Somme is home to 240 British and Commonwealth cemeteries, varying in size from Hunter's Cemetery with 46 graves to Serre Road Cemetery No. 2 with 7,127. Of these 7,127 men, only 2,183 are identified. The rest are 'known only unto God'. In addition, there are 22 French military cemeteries and 14 German. There was no repatriation of British war dead after 1915, hence the far greater number of British and Commonwealth cemeteries. Rancourt cemetery is the largest French war cemetery on the Somme, holding the remains of 8,566 men.

The Thiepval Memorial to the Missing of the Somme.

On 1 August 1932, Prince Edward, the Prince of Wales (the future Edward VIII), unveiled the Thiepval Memorial to the Missing of the Somme. The war memorial, a grand arch designed by Sir Edwin Lutyens, commemorates the 72,195 missing British and South African servicemen who died during the Battle of the Somme. Those from Australia, Canada, India, Newfoundland and New Zealand with no known grave are commemorated on national memorials to the missing at Villers-

Bretonneux, Vimy Ridge, Neuve Chapelle, Beaumont-Hamel and Longueval respectively.

On 29 January 1928, Douglas Haig died from a heart attack brought on, according to his widow, by the strain of wartime command. He was 66.

Haig is often remembered as the archetypal 'donkey' leading 'lions' to their death, but at war's end, he was hailed as a hero. His death saw much outpouring of public grief, especially in his hometown of Edinburgh, and London, where up to a million people turned out to pay their respects. The day of his funeral was declared a day of national mourning.

Haig's only son, Dawyck Haig, who was imprisoned in Colditz during the Second World War and who died in 2009, was a staunch defender of his father. In an interview for the BBC in June 2006, the eve of the 90th anniversary of the first day of the Somme, he said, 'He was not a brutish man, he was a very kind, wonderful man and by God, I miss him… I believe it has now turned full circle and people appreciate his contribution. But it saddens me my three sisters have not survived to see it. They died suffering from the beastly attitudes of the public towards our father'.

In 1937, a statue of Douglas Haig, the Earl Haig Memorial, was unveiled on London's Whitehall. Designed by sculptor, Alfred Frank Hardiman, and eight years in the making, it won many plaudits and prizes but unfortunately, the stance of the horse is that of one in the process of urinating.

The Earl Haig Memorial.

* * * * *

Images

All the images used in this book are, as far as I can ascertain, in the public domain. If I have mistakenly used an image that is not in the public domain, please let me know at rupert@historyinanhour.com and I shall remove / replace the offending item.

Other works by Rupert Colley:

Fiction:

This Time Tomorrow – 'Two brothers. One woman. A nation at war.' Part One of *The Searight Saga*, a compelling story of war, brotherly love, passion and betrayal during World War One. Vast in scope and intimate in the portrayal of three lives swept along by circumstances.

The Unforgiving Sea – 'Ten men adrift on a lifeboat. Only one will live to tell the tale.' Part Two of *The Searight Saga*. On its surface, a tale of murder, survival and loss set in World War Two, while at its core we find a story of deep love, loyalty and forgiveness.

The Woman on the Train – 'Someone saves your life. How far will you go to repay the debt?' A wartime debt threatens to ruin a musician's career and much more.

The White Venus – 'When the ties of loyalty are severed, whom do you trust?' Set in Nazi-occupied France during World War Two, a coming-of-age tale of divided loyalties, trust and a tragedy never forgotten but never mentioned.

The Black Maria – 'When love becomes your greatest enemy.' A love story set in 1930s Soviet Union, a novel about fear: fear of each other, fear of being denounced, fear of Stalin's secret police; and, ultimately, the fear of falling in love.

My Brother the Enemy – 'Fear on the streets. Death on every corner. But the real enemy is the brother at his side.' A story of jealousy, sibling rivalry and betrayal, and a desperate bid for freedom, set against the backdrop of Nazi oppression and war.

The Torn Flag – 'Sometimes the simplest of choices can have the most devastating of consequences.' Set during the Hungarian Revolution, an epic tale of people caught in the machinations of history, where the choices you make determine your fate.

The Sixth Man – 'Six prisoners. Five must die. Who will live?'
1944. A Nazi prison in France. Six French prisoners; five face execution. They have one night to decide who should live and who should die.

Non-fiction:

The 'History In An Hour' series
Published by HarperCollins.

The Savage Years: Tales From the 20th Century, a collection of sixty essays covering the two world wars, the Soviet Union, Nazi Germany, the Cold War, black history and much more.

A History of the World Cup
A history of football's ultimate competition.

Historyinanhour.com

Rupertcolley.com

Printed in Great Britain
by Amazon